THE MUSIC OF LIGHT REGRET

Poems by Louis Phillips

Published by World Audience, Inc.

©2021, Louis Phillips

ISBN: 9798761484672

The publisher and editor-in-chief of World Audience Publishers i
M. Stefan Strozier (www.mstefanstrozier.com).

"But the nun's words also spoke to a basic skill that many of us in Cannes were having to suddenly relearn: that of being outside in a body, in the world among all its perils."

—Jessica Kiang, "Falling Back in Love with Cannes" in *The New York Times* (July 19, 2021)

ACKNOWLEDGMENTS

"Some of the World is the World," "The Music of Light Regret," " A.M.," "Eight Feet Tall," "My Old Man Was A Terrible Swimmer," "My Wife Stands at Our Window," and "Music Begins Somewhere —all appeared originally in OFFCOURSE, edited by Isabel L. Nirenberg and Ricardo Nirenberg, to whom I owe a great debt.

For

Pat, Ian, Allie, &, of course, Mateo

& in memory of Matthew

CONTENTS

THE MUSIC OF LIGHT REGRET

The solar heart of Constantinople.
Where does that phrase come from?
Sleep places me inside her car.
When I awake I am in Athens.
I have never been to Greece,
Nor had my father whose own father

Had been born in Thessaloniki.
I shd have sent my parents there,
But I did not. Add another failure
To that decades old To-Do List.
My mother rarely saw her grandsons.
I stare out my window at statues

Of strange gods, at monuments
Crumbling under casting nets
Of Destiny/Fate, Cosmic Warfare.
I am not the only creature
Who licks the salt of old wounds.
Fragrance of past mistakes lingers
Within The Cathedral of Atoms.

A broad expanse of hurt spreads
Across our universe,
Losing energy, entropic
Freeze lockers of ghosts
& Time machines rusting
In parking lots. My sleeping car
Stutters into a foreign station.

Surrounded by big water,
So much of this deserted city
Bends under Attic heat,
Just as we all bend under weight
Of what has happened long ago,
Our past more changeable
Now & then than the present.

On dark water, a lone fisherman,
Like his fathers before him,
In a small skiff throws out his net,
A wide circle far from the boat,
Widening, not yet a ghost net,
Onto, into the ocean, vanishing.
The sun stalls below the horizon.

The Conductor enters my sleeping car,
The geography of dreaming:
No matter where I am
I cannot find my way back home.
The floating opera of the world
Floats by. What strange music,
What strange arias I awake to.

SOME OF THE WORLD IS THE WORLD

Prologue

July 16, 1945. Detonation
Of the first nuclear Bomb,
A plutonium implosion device,
Was exploded in New Mexico,
On the Jornada de Muerto.
Such immense power.
Our world will never be the same.

J. Robert Oppenheimer recites
A line from the Bhagavad Gita:
"Now I am become Death,
the destroyer of worlds." —Vishnu.

Is not the Past all Prologue?

1

August 6, 2020. Hiroshima.
75 yrs ago, the whitest flash
The world has ever seen,
City & children in flames,
Ashes on the doorsteps
& strict laws of radiation
Waiting to be obeyed.
Heat too hot to be imagined.
160,000 dead.
What scholars call History,
Ordinary people call Suffering.
What times have we lived thru.

2

Lao Tzu speaks to us:
Gravity is the root of grace.

3

I myself must be light-headed,
Thoughts containing more spin
Than gravity can contain.
Midnight. My head is spinning,
Fierce tales, pandemic thoughts:
Refrigerator trucks,

Parked on side streets for months,
Crammed to overflowing.
Bring up the bodies.

White caps in oceans of imaginings
Flow in, flow out,
Entire cities crushed, flooded,

Families mortally wounded.
Some of the world is the world,
Some of it is us.

4

It must be midnight somewhere.
Objects in my living room
Take on lives of their own.
The photo of my 5 yr old sons
In their Superman costumes,
Red capes flying,
Truth, Justice, & the American way.
Tell me another one.
One son alive. One son dead.
Bring up the bodies.
On the radio, Willie Nelson:
"Nothing I Can Do About It."

5

My wife's Japanese doll
Dressed in a kimono dances.
The World's bright Music
Takes me away from myself,
Our universe too
Pulses arpeggios of desires.
Do you not hear them?
Clusters of notes,
Scales of falling, Scales of rising,
Murmur of far away planets,
Followed by harmonic whispers.

6

My wife when she was 10
Lived in Japan
Where her father worked
For the State Department.
World War II
Was not far enough away.
Subways were filled
With maimed veterans,
Scarred soldiers, sailors.
Hana wa sakuragi, hito wa bushi.
When my wife's family
Went to the beach,
Japanese gathered around them
To stare at them:
Such pale blonde creatures.

7

What is the wind
Amid rhythmic change of seasons
On this planet singing now?
With so much gravity at stake,
Some worlds are filled
To the breaking point
Before they even come into being,
Some worlds are strange
Because they no longer exist,
Others are strange
Because of absence of water.
Some private worlds are strange
Because of absence.

8

Winds pick up. Hurricane.
My mother & I,
Working by candlelight,
Are covering with brown paper,
Cut up grocery bags,
3 volumes of a dictionary
I had lugged home from college.
I own more dictionaries
Than I can possibly use.
Words escape me. So many
Persons I loved have escaped me:
Son by 2 A.M. morning.
Mother by candlelight.

9

Whether I wish for God or not,
There is a magician's trick
Involving a box with a false bottom.
The universe is such a Pandora's Box,
An immense collection
Of spinning gravities,
With a false bottom of Hope.

10

Earth, its citizens remind me
Of lungless salamanders
Absorbing oxygen thru their skin.
Not once concerning themselves
With residual radiation.
Entire islands of energy
Turn upon themselves,
Dramatic patterns
Shake us up & down,
Bells ringing, an 8
On the Richter scale,
Seismic shifts of many lives,
Black holes of shimmy,
Plutonium flares at the core.
Little Boy. Little Boy.

August 9, 1945. Nagasaki.
75 yrs ago, the whitest flash
The world has ever seen,
City & children in flames,
Ashes on the doorsteps,
Handfuls of radiating dust,
Pebbles on the gravestones.
The Emperor of Japan in 1945:
"The war situation has developed
Not necessarily to Japan's advantage."
An explosion giving off
A temperature of 540,000 Fahrenheit.

80,000 to 120,000 dead.
Definitely a disadvantage.
165 *nijū hibakusha,*
Double explosion-affected people,
Persons who were bombed
In both Hiroshima & Nagasaki.

12

Does the universe have a center?

13

Bring up the body.
With help from Leonard,
My father's best friend,
& 4 others from the funeral home,
I removed my father's coffin
In the Florida heat, humidity,
To carry it to the gravesite.
The coffin, a well carved box.
No false bottom on this one.
Just one more black hole
That will not shimmy.
Some deaths deeper than others.
Lower the body with ropes
Six feet down. 2 yards.
A handful of sand, pebbles,
My mother, my sisters,
Myself with fresh tears.
Private histories, Public histories
Shake us up & down,
Which shakes us to the core?
Years later, I return to this place.
My sister & I wander
For nearly a half hour
Under a scorching sun:
Just where was the old man buried?

14

The Quick and the Dead.
But what about the dying?
They are neither quick
Nor dead. The old saying:
There are the living
& the dead & those at sea.
Survivors gather
At the edge of the ocean
With its surge of savage waves.
Tidal barons ruling the roost.
Bonfires on the beach.

A lone musician strums a guitar,
Whisper sings Malvina Reynold's
Little boxes on the hillside
Little boxes all the same.
Nightmares. Survivors' nightmares.
Step into the box and disappear.
Vaporized.

AT THIS TIME OF YEAR, ALL HELL BREAKS LOOSE

With non-passive voices of spring,
All hell breaks loose.
Startled by bristling winds,
The green world splits to blossom
With evasive buddings. Hah!
The bark & peel of landscape
Enlarges to be seen, *la la la*.
No human gesture carries weight
Amid such damp connivings.

"THE SHINING WINGS ON WHICH
THE DRAGONFLY RIDES"

From the deck of my in-laws' country house I watch
A wet-meadow dragonfly of the genus *Sympetrum*,
How honest it is,
Taking only what it needs.
The sun means the world to it.
I wonder why I get up in the morning.
My younger 40 yr. old sister's phone has been disconnected,
So I have to call her at work.
She says We get older, we learn from experience,
But still we die stupid.
Wisdom, I suppose, meaning;
We do not trust, the way we used to, other human beings.
So many human values, false values.
I tell her I find the phrase
Waste not, want not, troubling.
The rich have so much to waste,
Yet they are not the ones in want,
While the poor have nothing to waste.
Imagine dragonflies on the telephone,
Calling from office phones:
"Meet you in the meadow at 10 A.M."
There they go: the dragonflies!
Black-faced skimmers, yellow wings.
For them, life must be more simple,
Their shadows nothing but a vein of wings.

A MURDER OF CROWS

Halfway up heaven,
A full spectrum of crows

Cacophony of lost causes,
Caws, caws,

& not one of the bastards
Thinks about me.

MUSIC BEGINS SOMEWHERE

"...no language has been invented comprehensible
to both the living and the dead." —Czeslaw Milosz

Not always in the throat.
Perhaps when we hear
A murder of crows in flight,
Or spy a rowboat,

Hearing the clink of metal
When oars are fitted
Into the oarlocks as we settle
Onto the thwarts.

Music begins
When we set forth on a journey
Becoming more than alive.
Thru raven-riven woods

On a path leading to a pub,
Or to a church,
Or, more happily, to home,
Music quickens the pace

The climb may be steep,
Weather may refuse
To cooperate. Of course, maps
Are of absolutely no use

To any person who travels
Only in his sleep.
The same might be sd
Of music, although mourners

Often open a hymnal
And offer a chorus
To usher the newly dead
Into another world.

A WALK ALONG THE SHORE

A few miles north of Cape May.
Along the Atlantic Shore,
The wordless ocean
Pushes or pulls us toward/away

Into a more profound way
Of sensing depth & pitch
Of places, persons, animals
Far beyond our reach. Play

Of sunlight upon the waves
Teases us, invites us in,
But, we must turn away,
Return home. What to say?

Home. Even if we we stay
Far from water, far
From where we once were,
Our thoughts, turning this way

& that, return to that day
When someone disappeared,
One gone in a flash,
Without a cry, without a word,

When Death became mere formality.

MY WIFE STANDS AT OUR BEDROOM WINDOW

My wife stands at our bedroom window.
Where is the moon,
What have we done with it?
It was here yesterday. Where did it go?
When you are married
For as many years as we have been
So many persons, objects,
Astronomical events become neglected.
Perhaps she is counting red taillights
Of an endless line of cars
Crawling like snail to New Jersey.
Never has the George Washington Bridge,
Next to Venus, been so far away.
Or is she straining her eyesight,
Looking for our dead son
Walking on the sidewalks,
Waving to her, 14 stories up?
What are you looking at?
Christmas lights strung
Along tops of buildings across the street.
Come away from the window.

No, she says, you must see this.
What? A full moon. There.
By the water tower.
In the end, our lives
Come down to light.

3 A.M.

Waiting up for my sons to return,
Breathing six packs of beer
From whatever braveries
They have set for themselves,
From whatever breweries
They have put out of business.
I watch the tiny hands
Of the bedroom clock advance,
Until, at last, I hear
The front door open. I glance
To that side of the bed
Where my wife turns, sleeps,
Breathing in & out
Upon some farther shore.
I think: How much better it is
To turn the darkness inside out
& make it dance
Rather than to lie down in fear.

POET RUN OVER BY STEAMROLLER

Marianne Moore juxtaposed
A butterfly upon a steamroller,
But this is not that poem.
This is about
The largest steamroller of them all.

I lie down under Grief
& presses me flat.
Need I remind you of that old joke:
"Lady, your son has just been
Run over by a steamroller.

What shall we do with his body?"
"Slide him under the door."

OLD AGE

With lives beyond my claiming,
I board a Greyhound Bus.
Heading for my lost Woodstock,
Slapdash fodledoodle. Clocks

Say 3:15, A.M. P.M. PMS?
I take a bus heading
In the wrong direction,
West instead of North.

What day is it, *et. al., etc.*
Found out too late. Just my luck:
"By the time we got to Woodstock
We were half a million strong.'

Every one of a certain age
Understands: fast or slow,
No matter where you go
By land, sea, or air,

You're gonna end up somewhere.

2 A.M.

Like some frightened creature,
Am stymied
In a dark that has no end to it.
The Earth I know
Spins at great speed,
But, at this late hour,

Staggering from bar to bar,
I am not tossed off.
Wandering
Within a Forest of Loss,
It is comforting to know
The Universe & I

Are headed in the same direction.

IN MEDIA RES

Let me start in the middle of things.
Why not,
We are always in the middle of things.

Were you in the middle of something?
I don't mean
To interrupt. Continue with something

To do, but no matter what you do
There is more
To be done. What else can we do,

Running from one chore to another?
You amid
Some intimate drama or another,

While I try to hold your attention
For a few minutes.
Pause, Now a let-down of attention

Until the pipes & tumbrels of time
Call us away,
Suspended as we are for a brief time

Between the beginning & the end.

SOMEPLACE ELSE

How many more mornings
Dare I cross off
From Mortality's calendar?

How many times
Shall I lie awake
Next to my wife of nearly 50 yrs,

Thinking impossible thoughts?
No matter where I am
Or might be,

There is always someplace else.

W. H. AUDEN ALONE IN A MOTEL IN OREGON

"I'll have my sixtieth birthday alone in an Oregon motel."
—W. H. Auden

Hours after a brief lecture on *Tartuffe,*
& its characters, Elmire & Orgon,
The major poet
Retires to a major motel in Oregon
(A Howard Johnson's with its orange roof).

If old age is a country, many citizens
No longer vote & many more are gone.
On the radio,
Historians discuss the Battle of the Argonne
Forest. A bottle of gin? It's in

One of his bags. 60! Happy Birthday!
An ungodly time to get one's life organ-
ized. Think ahead.
Lonely & 60 & one's death a foregone
Conclusion. What's one life worth? Say,

Is it better to live, poor, honest, & aloof?
Should I invest in art like J.P. Morgan?
A major poet
In a minor key. *What did I lecture on?*
Oh, yes. I remember now Tartuffe.

THE DESERTED HOUSE

Never once thanking me.
Half-naked cardinals
Filagree the feeder,

Seedlings overlapping
With blacktailed doe,
Summer whizzes by so fast.
I scarcely believe it,

Then four black kittens
Who live under
The deserted house next door
Wait in the bushes,
Demanding to be fed,

My sons bob & weave
With broken branches
Stuck inside their shorts:
"Guns," they say'
On their way to shoot somebody.

Squirrels leap
From tree trunks
To my window ledge.
By the time I feed everybody
The day is half over.

Apple sized full frontal
Mornings meandering
To nowhere.
Swaddled in weakness,
Empires collapse,
Cities fall, while
White comass skirting tangles
Sighs. I have lived
More than 70 summers,

But none of them are here.

MODESTY SONGS

I am so lathered by time,
When I enter a room
Women don't look up,

But in another place
I remember
Red petticoats shimmering

& a low-class girl
Who got under my skin,
& I under her skin.

Sure, I am half-way
Between the pulpit
& a coroner's report,

But she gave me
The pleasantest night
That ever passed over my head.

O sweet ladies,
Don't glance up from your stitching.
Please don't stop singing

Your modesty songs
For my sake.

WHAT SORT OF PLACE THE WORLD IS

Weather & luck both turn
Today the winter is long gone
With so many awakenings,
Many humans more mysterious
Than Stonehenge.

Only in one's imagination
Do trees grow upside down,
Their thick roots in the air.
Then comes light, then darkness,
Then going home.

WHAT THE WORLD IS LIKE NOW

Elegant winds bow & scrape
Thru stands of sycamores.
People held in thrall
By music in leaves come & go.

I could start there, but I won't.
As soon as humans enter
Too much pain,
Misunderstandings.
No, I shall start

With stars shredded
By gravity. Bone tides.
We are, each of us, pulled
'This way & that. I have a life,

But do not know
What I have. Mortality
On the half-shell,
Whispering "Life is all you have,
But you have Death too."

Amid swirl, whirl, & sweep
Of flowing seasons
There comes time to let go.
All such loveliness lost
& a host of feelings
Like faraway stars shredded,
Sunlight falls thru the days
As if the days never existed,
While our Earth,

Deep delved, enchanted spins.

THUNDERSTRUCK

Under summer's
Heavy shadow,
There is more rain
Than we can shake a stick at:

Night rain tattooing
A cabin's roof,
Fallout from planets
Without atmosphere,

Fog rain
Tapping lightly
Upon kingdoms of windows.
False rain,

True rain, true or false rain
Ending a drought,
Drowning wild turkeys
With opened throats,

Choral rains, chanting
Umbrella requiems,
Symphonic rains
Celebrating creation,

Animal rains soaking
Fur, soothing
Hallelujah
Spiritual rain,

Water be praised!
Secular down pouring
Outpouring
Of inner weather

Thunderstruck.

WHAT ELSE IS SUMMER FOR?

I had picked wild roses by the firehouse,
But one inexhaustible blossom
Had fallen from my bicycle basket.

I was all the way home
With smell of twilight on the lake
When I discovered what was missing.

2 miles. I biked all the way back
To find it by the side of the road.
What else is summer for?

TRAGOS ODE

Goat song.
In the crawlspace of love
'The lust of a goat
Was, right or wrong,

Within me.
For a brief breathing space
Among the lasses, alas!
Nothing wd be

Otherwise.
Now, grabble & sprawl
Of seasons are upon me.
Swallows in the joe-pie

Weeds, sway
of holy ghosts, the years,
As they say,
Have had their way

With me.
On the hillside, young girls
Rustle their skirts
& laugh & up the scree

Goats capering,
Jumping onto & over,
Then into fields,
Not amazed, nor wondering

How even
Our deepest loves
Cannot save us
From ourselves.

NIGHT BLINDNESS

Even as the disc
Of the moon
Flattens its head
Amid a bed of little woes,
I travel into nightfall
Only to return
With heaps of it.
I see with my heart
I see my own
Inability to see.
Even as you touch me now,
I am aware
Of thousands of kisses
That will never happen.

MOTHER

Pinks reign like roadside kings,
But butter-and-eggs &
Beggar's jewels hold my affection.

End of summer.
Those terrifying words,
With music in half-
Completed houses so loud
I hear it in the blackberry bushes
Where I pretend
To be Robinson Crusoe
Feasting on berries,

My hands stained with juice.
This morning
Nature is my big-hearted mama,
Tomorrow she will send cold rain.
When I turn to her again,
She will say:
"Don't come whining to me."

THERE IS ALWAYS A SHIP SAILING
SOMEWHERE OVER CRAZY WEEDS

Lifting up the skirts
Of the cheerfully invisible.
My life is never so bad
As I make it seem.
It is, however, a mess,
Of feelings & unpaid bills,
Gods grinding & grinding,
Making mash of my days.

Of course, there is the sense
That someone is missing.
Every day someone vanishes,
900 immigrants
Falling off a boat, capsizing,
Drowning. But what's the sense
In holding back?
There is always a ship sailing

Somewhere over crazy weeds.
Wind takes the sails & we go.
Few persons insist that Life,
Textured with yearnings,
Has to last so many yrs
Or that we must forgive
All the cruelties laid upon us.
Each day contains some act
That will not be tidy.

FURYU NO ASOBI

The puzzle of reading poetry:
Readers take this poem apart,
Rebuild each line with new &
Different words. Many years later,
The original words are found.
A second poem is constructed.
Which was original poem?

The answer is easy:

The one that harbors
The most eloquent silence.

EIGHT FEET TALL

"Man, I'm buoyant. I feel about eight feet tall." —Frank Sinatra

Because the world
Bulges at the seams,
We learn ideas
Only to unlearn them.
Coming off the stage,
Frank Sinatra announces
He feels 8 feet tall.
Is it a blessing not many
Of us are ever that tall?
Frankenstein's monster
Was taller than Sinatra,
But his height
Brought him little comfort.
Then there was the man
In a Diane Arbus photo,
Towering over his parents
Robert Wadlow, 8'11.
In Turkey, Sul
Checks in at 8' 2",
The tallest living person.
We also know the story
Of Goliath & David,
How at 6 cubits
& a span he towered
Over a diminutive David,
Underscoring some moral
So easy to ignore.

My grandmother wd say
"Don't get too big
For your britches."
In my old age, I have grown
Too big for my britches,
But I'm not 8 feet tall,
Not by a long shot.
I am, in fact, shrinking,
Yet on the afternoon
When I watched my wife
Give birth to twin sons,
Their vocal entrances,
I was then the tallest man
In the universe.

MY OLD MAN WAS A TERRIBLE SWIMMER

Watching my mother
Doing the backstroke
Throughout my childhood
Was better than watching
Esther Williams
Dropping from a trapeze,
Falling through billowing smoke
Into her own M-G-M pool
Filled with bathing beauties.
My mother's swimming
Made the Atlantic Ocean
Of my growing up
A world of casual grace.
My old man, on the other hand,
Was a terrible swimmer,
A few awkward strokes,
Swamped by waves,
& he struggled back to the beach.
My mother cd outswim him
By at least 30,000 miles.
Today, as I near 80,
I am becoming my father,
Same pains in my left leg.
My wife swims like my mother,
While I splash the water
Mercilessly, awkwardly,
Chlorine in my mouth,
Plugs for my ears.
Pat goes 20 laps

To my 3 and a half.
I stand by the side of the pool
& try to remember
The sound of my parents' voices.

YOU CAN'T GET THERE FROM HERE

Happiness. Pop 302.
You can drive
From one end of town to the other
In a matter of seconds

Can't buy a clean pair of slacks
At the General Store
& the One Joy Cafe
Is always out of one thing or another.

No booze. No drugs.
No railroad tracks. No airfields.
Travel agents are useless
No nothing for whatever moves.

Main Street for centuries
Yawns unrepaired
Side streets are Dead Ends.
Potholes larger than the moon.
Bridges near the city limits
Have collapsed.

You can't get there from here.
Don't even try.

BETTER THAN READING THIS POEM

Better reading this poem
Is breathing a midsummer's
Stripped–to-the-bone moonlight,

Allowing us to ponder
What is visible & invisible
In the many moistures of love.

Better than reading this poem
Is keeping
All the lights of the spirit on.

KNOWING HOW NATURE IS

"You know how nature is, even in the movies" —*William Saroyan*

Nature: What fine petticoats she wears.
Better-lined than any woman I know
With a body to take you by storm,
Bosh on her slopes.
What high-skirt dancing
When she shows off sexual paraphernalia
Of a very high order.
Toi o lai nha mot nguoi ban::
So many languages she speaks,
Hotsy-totsy with her bedroom eyes,
But doesn't give a damn in any of them.
Nature: What a blowjob she gives you.
All you can do is lie on your bed,
Your life scattered around you,
Naked, exhausted, & thankful

WHAT I MISS MOST

At odds with mind's hunger
Or soul's rage,
"One's body, too, is so lonely."

I came crying into this world
With its gods
& knew I was overmatched,

But tonight I miss most
The elegance
Of your own body's loneliness,

That takes me in at once,
When suddenly
I touch your breasts

Rounder than Giotto's O's.

ILIUM

Life is short. Toss
Another cliché' into the barrel of loss.
My body is a 5' 8"'Greek epic
Of aches & bruises,
As if I have been fighting in Troy
For nearly 80 yrs,
Standing toe to heel
With the young Achilles,
Awaiting the arrival of a magic horse.
Each morning I emerge,
Armed, unarmed,
Into a whirlwind of conflicts,
Hand to hand combat.
I wonder how much courage I have left.

THERE ARE THESE LONG COMMUTES

There are these long commutes.
You get on a train &
The train is crowded. You
Realize that the train
Is not going anywhere, &
Your life is not going anywhere, &
That is the longest commute of all.

THE WORLD'S BODY

"Charles made love to me. What you might call a farewell fuck."
—Evelyn Keyes, Scarlett O'Hara's Younger Sister

Thunder squall,
Then flash.
The Past in motion.
Microseconds zero to nothing.

Nothing will come of nothing.
Who said that? Some loser?
Oh well, even kings
Can be losers.

A torrent of days
Opening & closing,
On lives
Beginning & ending.

My grandson cries
& we leap to our feet.
A new generations
Take to the field,

Renewing
Our world's body
Which is not my body.
My body has survived

Seven decades,
Long-tailed
English warblers
Have long ago abandoned

The meadows,
But the scent of autumn
Lingers on the wind.
The seasons

Are head over heels
In farewells,
Friend & relatives
Dying on schedule

Or out of turn,
Comings & goings.
Down mountains
Through corridors of Spain,

Across the Atlantic,
Tramontava
From the Pyrenees,
A south wind called Garbi.

Who names the winds?
Not many gods
Are allowed
To name the winds.

Fogfall, frostbow, tidefall.
It is not the winds,
Nor tides
That shake my bones,

It's the state of loss
That shivers my timbers,
Whittles me
Into an artifact

Easily forgotten.
Wherever winds flow
From here to there,
There to here,

They are simply saying
 Good-bye,
Farewell to places
I have never heard of.

ABOUT THE AUTHOR

Louis Phillips, a widely published poet, playwright, and short story writer, has written some 50 books for children and adults. Among his published works are: six collections of short stories – *A Dream of Countries Where No One Dare Live* (SMU Press), *The Bus to the Moon* (Fort Schuyler Press), *The Woman Who Wrote King Lear and Other Stories* (Pleasure Boat Studio), *Must I Weep for The Dancing Bear* (Pleasure Boat Studio), *Galahad in the City of Tigers*, and *Sheathed Bayonets* (World Audience). *Hot Corner*, a collection of his baseball writings, and *R.I.P.* (a sequence of poems about Rip Van Winkle) from Livingston Press; *The Envoi Messages, The Ballroom in St. Patrick's Cathedral* and *The Last of The Marx Brothers' Writers*, full-length plays, (Broadway Play Publishers). *Fireworks in Some Particulars* (Fort Schuyler Press) is a collection of poetry, short stores, and humor pieces. That book also contains his play – *God Have Mercy on the June-Bug*. Pleasure Boat Studio has published *The Domain of Silence/The Domain of Absence: New & Selected Poems*, and *The Domain Of Small Mercies: New & Selected Poems*. Read more about Louis Phillips' numerous World Audience books on his Wikipedia page or his web site: www.louis-phillips.com.

BOOKS BY LOUIS PHILLIPS PUBLISHED BY WORLD AUDIENCE PUBLISHERS

The Audience Book of Theater Quotations
American Elegies (poems)
The Death of the Siamese Twins & Other Plays
The Kilroy Sonata (poems)
Hollywood Scandals (plays)
The Moon Nobody Wanted
Honduras & Other Plays
Late Night in the Rain Forest (play)
The Collaborators (play)
The Secret Voyage of Melvin Moonmist
The Last Lion
Robot 9 in Wonderland
How Wide the Meadow (poems)
Caesar, Caesar, Caesar (play)
Narragansett 1937 (play)
Dr. Jazz: A Comedy (play)
Canary in the Mine: A Collection of Humor
Galahad in the City of Tigers (short stories)
Quick Flicks (clerihews)
The Pleasure of His Company (the off-beat Shakespeare book)
Dial M for Mysteries
The Oarsmen & Other Plays
Icebergs and Other Plays
Rowing to the Silly Islands (light verse)
It Takes a Lot of Paper to Gift Wrap an Elephant (children's book)
Sheathed Bayonets & Other Stories
4 (stories, plays, poems)
Procession (a film script)
Sentenced (Reading, Writing, and Book Publishing)
La Triviata: The Book of Off-Beat Fun Quizzes (first edition; second edition)
The Book of Epigraphs

WORLD AUDIENCE PUBLISHERS
www.worldaudience.org

Made in the USA
Middletown, DE
24 December 2021